Alexander Graham Bell

Jennifer Strand

abdopublishing.com

Published by Abdo Zoom™, PO Box 398166, Minneapolis, Minnesota 55439. Copyright © 2017 by Abdo Consulting Group, Inc. International copyrights reserved in all countries. No part of this book may be reproduced in any form without written permission from the publisher. Abdo Zoom™ is a trademark and logo of Abdo Consulting Group, Inc.

Printed in the United States of America, North Mankato, Minnesota
072016
092016

THIS BOOK CONTAINS
RECYCLED MATERIALS

Cover Photo: Harris & Ewing/Library of Congress
Interior Photos: Harris & Ewing/Library of Congress, 1, 4; Detroit Publishing Co./Library of Congress, 5; iStockphoto, 6–7; Everett Historical/Shutterstock Images, 7, 17, 19; Science & Society Picture Library/Getty Images, 8, 10; Timoléon Lobrichon/Library of Congress, 9; Library of Congress, 11; Bettmann/Getty Images, 12, 13; North Wind Picture Archives, 15; Shutterstock Images, 16; Richard W. Sears/Library of Congress, 18

Editor: Emily Temple
Series Designer: Madeline Berger
Art Direction: Dorothy Toth

Publisher's Cataloging-in-Publication Data
Names: Strand, Jennifer, author.
Title: Alexander Graham Bell / by Jennifer Strand.
Description: Minneapolis, MN : Abdo Zoom, [2017] | Series: Incredible inventors
    | Includes bibliographical references and index.
Identifiers: LCCN 2016941399 | ISBN 9781680792270 (lib. bdg.) |
    ISBN 9781680793956 (ebook) | 9781680794847 (Read-to-me ebook)
Subjects: LCSH: Bell, Alexander Graham, 1847-1922--Juvenile literature. |
    Inventors--United States--Biography--Juvenile literature. | Telephone--
    United States--History--Juvenile literature.
Classification: DDC 621.385092 [B]--dc23
LC record available at http://lccn.loc.gov/2016941399

Table of Contents

Introduction. 4

Early Life. 6

Leader. 8

History Maker 10

Legacy. 16

Quick Stats. 20

Key Dates 21

Glossary 22

Booklinks 23

Index 24

Introduction

Alexander Graham Bell
was an inventor.

He made the first working telephone.

THIS MODEL OF BELL'S FIRST TELEPHONE IS A DUPLICATE OF THE INSTRUMENT THROUGH WHICH SPEECH SOUNDS WERE FIRST TRANSMITTED ELECTRICALLY, 1875.

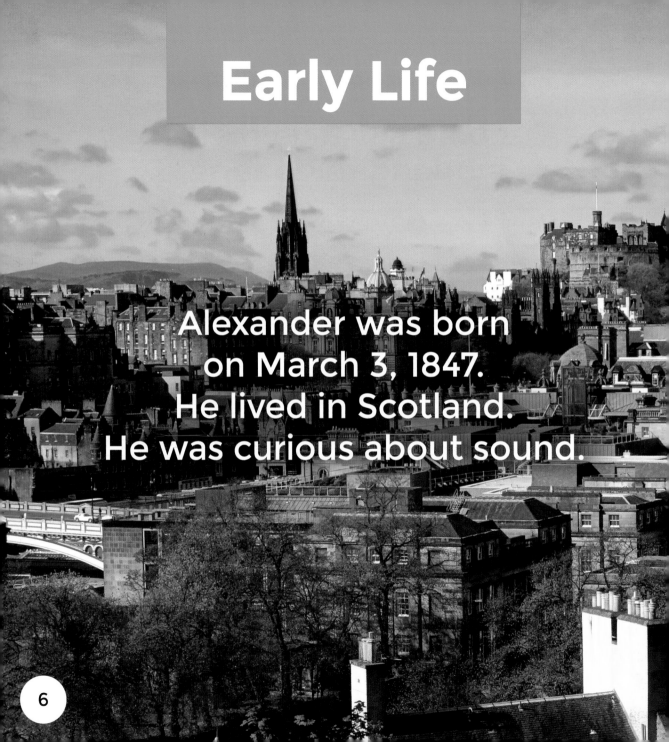

Early Life

Alexander was born
on March 3, 1847.
He lived in Scotland.
He was curious about sound.

He made a robot head.
It could say a few words.

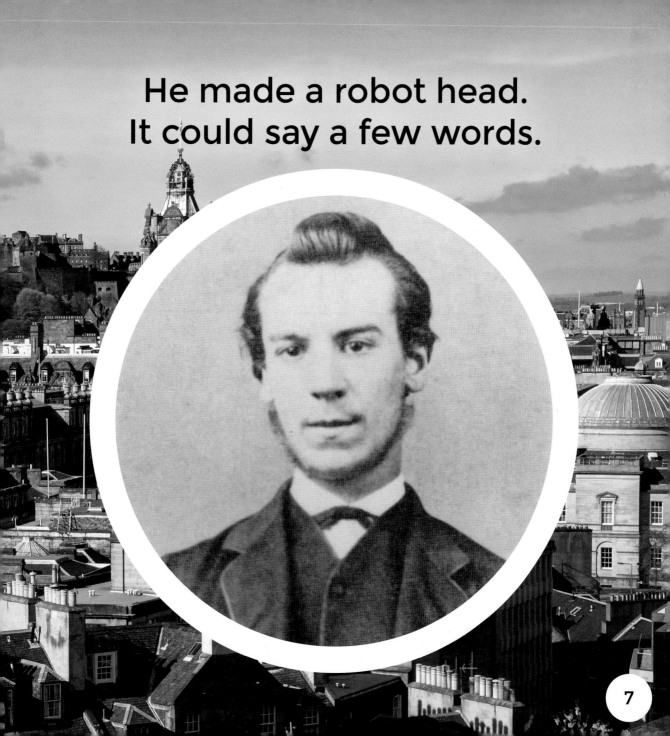

Leader

Bell made the **telegraph** better.
He used **reeds**.

They made sounds.
The sounds went over a wire.

Bell wanted to send
the sound of a voice.

He and Thomas Watson made
a machine. It used a membrane.
The membrane would vibrate.

They added a **funnel**. It pointed sound at the membrane. It connected to another machine. They could hear each other speak from one machine to the other.

Their telephone worked.

Later Bell made the first telephone call across the United States. He was in New York. He called someone in California.

Legacy

Many people had tried to make a machine to talk through.

But Bell made the first
working telephone.

Telephones were important.

They made communication easier. It became faster too.

Bell died on August 2, 1922.

Quick Stats

Alexander Graham Bell

Born: March 3, 1847

Birthplace: Edinburgh, Scotland, United Kingdom

Wife: Mabel Hubbard

Known For: Bell invented the telephone.

Died: August 2, 1922

Key  Dates

1847: Alexander Graham Bell is born on March 3.

1870: The Bell family moves to Canada.

1871: Bell begins teaching deaf students.

1874-1876: Bell and Thomas Watson work to create the telephone.

1915: Bell makes the first call across the United States.

1922: Bell dies on August 2.

Glossary

communication - the sharing of information.

funnel - a hollow, cone-shaped instrument.

membrane - a thin, flexible sheet.

reed - a thin, flexible strip of wood, metal, or plastic.

telegraph - a machine that carries coded messages over wires.

vibrate - to make very small, quick movements back and forth.

Booklinks

For more information on
Alexander Graham Bell, please visit
booklinks.abdopublishing.com

Learn even more with the Abdo Zoom
Biographies database. Check out
abdozoom.com for more information.

Index

born, 6

California, 14

call, 14

died, 19

funnel, 12

membrane, 11, 12

New York, 14

reeds, 8

robot, 7

Scotland, 6

telegraph, 8

telephone, 5, 13, 14, 16, 18

Watson, Thomas, 11